PSALMS II

Praying
with Jesu

A Guided Discovery for Groups and Individuals

Kevin Perrotta

LOYOLAPRESS.
CHICAGO

LOYOLAPRESS.

3441 N. ASHLAND AVENUE
CHICAGO, ILLINOIS 60657
(800) 621-1008
WWW.LOYOLABOOKS.ORG

Nihil Obstat
Reverend John Lodge, S.S.L., S.T.D.
Censor Deputatus
November 27, 2002

Imprimatur
Most Reverend Raymond E. Goedert, M.A., S.T.L., J.C.L.
Vicar General
Archdiocese of Chicago
December 4, 2002

The *Nihil Obstat* and *Imprimatur* are official declarations that a book is free of doctrinal and moral error. No implication is contained therein that those who have granted the *Nihil Obstat* and *Imprimatur* agree with the content, opinions, or statements expressed. Nor do they assume any legal responsibility associated with publication.

The Scripture quotations contained herein are from the New Revised Standard Version Bible: Catholic Edition, copyright © 1993 and 1989 by the Division of Christian Education of the National Council of the Churches of Christ in the U.S.A. Used by permission. All rights reserved. Subheadings in Scripture quotations have been added by Kevin Perrotta.

The story of Bilquis Sheikh (p. 19) is drawn from her autobiographical account, *I Dared to Call Him Father* (Grand Rapids, Mich.: Baker Book House, 1978).

The quotations about the Ugandan martyrs (p. 29) are from Barry M. Coldrey, *The Martyrs of Uganda* (Thornbury, Victoria, Australia: Tamanaraik Press, 2001) and J. P. Thoonen, *Black Martyrs* (New York: Sheed and Ward, 1941).

The Latin text of St. Robert Bellarmine's commentary on Psalm 69 (p. 59) may be found in Cornelii a Lapide, S.J., *Roberti Bellarmini Explanatio in Psalmos,* Supplementum ad Commentaria in Scripturam Sacram, Tomus Primus (Paris: Louis Vivès, 1877), 438–51. Translation by Kevin Perrotta.

St. Augustine's remarks on Psalm 22 (p. 71) are drawn largely from his *Expositions on the Book of Psalms,* A Select Library of the Nicene and Post-Nicene Fathers of the Christian Church, vol. 8, trans. A. Cleveland Coxe (Grand Rapids, Mich.: W. B. Eerdmans, 1989). Translation modified for this guide by Kevin Perrotta.

Interior design by Kay Hartmann/Communique Design
Illustration by Charise Mericle Harper

ISBN 0-8294-1570-X

Printed in the United States of America
03 04 05 06 07 Bang 10 9 8 7 6 5 4 3 2 1

Contents

How to Use This Guide

You might compare the Bible to a national park. The park is so large that you could spend months, even years, getting to know it. But a brief visit, if carefully planned, can be enjoyable and worthwhile. In a few hours you can drive through the park and pull over at a handful of sites. At each stop you can get out of the car, take a short trail through the woods, listen to the wind blowing through the trees, get a feel for the place.

In this booklet we will read six of the psalms that played a prominent role in Jesus' life, along with the Gospel passages in which the psalms are quoted. We will take a leisurely walk through each of the psalms and Gospel excerpts, thinking carefully about what we are reading and what it means for our lives today. Although the Scripture readings are short, they will give us a great deal to reflect on. The psalms teach us about prayer and about God's saving plan for us, and the Gospel passages focus on Jesus in a way that illuminates who he is and what he has done for us.

This guide provides everything you need to explore these biblical readings in six discussions—or to do a six-part exploration on your own. The introduction on page 6 will prepare you to get the most out of your reading. The weekly sections provide explanations that highlight what the psalms mean for us today. Equally important, each section supplies questions that will launch your group into fruitful discussion, helping you to both investigate the readings for yourself and learn from one another. If you're using the booklet by yourself, the questions will spur your personal reflection.

Each discussion is meant to be a *guided discovery.*

Guided. None of us is equipped to read the Bible without help. We read the Bible *for* ourselves but not *by* ourselves. Scripture was written to be understood and applied in the community of faith. So each week "A Guide to the Reading," drawing on the work of both modern biblical scholars and Christian writers of the past, supplies background and explanations. The guide will help you grasp the message of the psalms and the Gospel readings. Think of it as a friendly park ranger who points out noteworthy details and explains what you're looking at so you can appreciate things for yourself.

4

Discovery. The purpose is for *you* to interact with the psalms and the Gospel accounts of Jesus. "Questions for Careful Reading" is a tool to help you dig into the text and examine it carefully. "Questions for Application" will help you consider what these words mean for your life here and now. Each week concludes with an "Approach to Prayer" section that helps you respond to God's word. Supplementary "Living Tradition" and "Saints in the Making" sections offer the thoughts and experiences of Christians past and present. By showing what the Scriptures have meant to others, these sections will help you consider what they mean for you.

How long are the discussion sessions? We've assumed you will have about an hour and a half when you get together. If you have less time, you'll find that most of the elements can be shortened somewhat.

Is homework necessary? You will get the most out of your discussions if you read the weekly material and prepare your answers to the questions in advance of each meeting.

What about leadership? If you happen to have a world-class biblical scholar in your group, by all means ask him or her to lead the discussions. But in the absence of any professional Scripture scholars, or even accomplished amateur biblical scholars, you can still have a first-class Bible discussion. Choose two or three people to take turns as facilitators, and have everyone read "Suggestions for Bible Discussion Groups" (page 76) before beginning.

Does everyone need a guide? a Bible? Everyone in the group will need their own copy of this booklet. It contains the text of the psalms and Gospel passages that are the focus of the sessions, so a Bible is not absolutely necessary—but each participant will find it useful to have one. You should have at least one Bible on hand for your discussions. (See page 80 for recommendations.)

How do we get started? Before you begin, take a look at the suggestions for Bible discussion groups (page 76) or individuals (page 79).

The Book of Psalms: Jesus Was Here

Surrounded by apartment buildings and busy streets, golden wheat shimmers in the June sun. Traces of centuries-old terraces, constructed to hold soil for olive trees, protrude from the scant vegetation on the hillside. A large, shallow depression carved into a flat rock in the ground—a grape press—testifies to a long-vanished vineyard. This small, undeveloped parcel of land close to the center of modern Nazareth is all that remains of the farmland of the first-century village. As a boy, Jesus probably scampered up and down these terraces. As a young man, he may have trampled grapes in the press with his relatives and neighbors.

Pilgrims travel great distances to stand at this spot. They wish to see where Jesus lived, to walk where he walked. For the same reason, they go to sit in the ruins of the synagogue in Capernaum where he preached, to drink a cup of water from the well in Nablus where he conversed with a Samaritan woman, to climb the steps by which he entered the temple in Jerusalem. The pilgrims have read the Gospels; coming here, they are impressed with the reality of it all. When they go home, they read the accounts of Jesus with deeper understanding.

The land of Israel and Palestine speaks so eloquently about Jesus that it has been called the Fifth Gospel. The ancient stones bear witness to the way of life, the possibilities, the hardships of his day. Yet, literally, the stones are mute. Wordless clues, they show us what the people of the time did, not what they thought. Gazing at the remnants of the orchard, the pilgrim to Nazareth may wonder whether there is any way to enter the minds of the people who built these terraces and lit their lamps from the oil of the olive trees they planted here. Is there, especially, any access to the thoughts of Jesus as he grew here from boyhood to manhood in preparation for his mission?

In one sense, the answer is no. Jesus left no memoirs. The Gospel writers give us no record of his thoughts during the years he lived in his hometown. Yet we *do* have some idea of what he thought about, for we have his Bible—the part of the Bible that Christians call the Old Testament. As a Jew, Jesus pondered Scripture. Judging from his frequent references to the psalms in his teaching and discussions, he gave particular attention to the book of Psalms.

Jesus would have learned to pray the psalms in the village synagogue and at home with Mary and Joseph. He would have chanted the psalms with the crowds of festival-goers in the temple in Jerusalem. It is reasonable to suppose that the psalms were in his mind and heart from his boyhood in Nazareth to his baptism at the Jordan, from the beginning of his ministry beside the Sea of Galilee to his final moments at Golgotha.

If we wish to get in touch with Jesus' thoughts and prayers, then, we can read the psalms. Opening the book of Psalms, we know that "Jesus was here."

We may assume that Jesus prayed all 150 psalms in the book of Psalms. But he seems to have focused his attention in a special way on a limited number of psalms (see "Jesus' Favorite Psalms," page 72). In this guide we will explore six of these psalms, with the Gospel passages in which they are quoted.

Our goal is twofold. We seek to understand Jesus better by examining prayers that were especially important to him. And we seek to grasp how we can use these psalms as our own prayer, given their connection with Jesus.

The goal line is clearly in view, but advancing the ball down the field for a touchdown is going to take some work and a combination of plays. The reason is that we need to explore the psalms on three levels of meaning. Our *first* task is to examine the meanings of the psalms in their Old Testament setting. These are the meanings that Jewish people in the time of Jesus would have found in the psalms; they are the meanings of the psalms as they came to Jesus. *Second,* we must look at the Gospel episodes in which the psalms are quoted, seeking to understand the psalms' deeper meaning as Jesus shows their connections with himself. But our exploration is not complete until, *third,* we consider how we can pray these psalms as reminders and celebrations of Jesus.

The process can be illustrated by looking ahead to our examination of Psalm 110. We will first explore the meanings of this psalm as an affirmation of God's support for the king of Israel and as a foreshadowing of a greater king to be sent by God to his people. Then we will observe how Jesus uses this psalm to assert his identity as the greater-than-expected king whom God has sent. Finally, we will reflect on how we can now pray this psalm as an acclamation of Jesus as risen Lord.

Obviously, this is a demanding program of exploration! In the course of our investigations, you may feel a little out of breath. Allow me to offer a couple of suggestions.

First, don't get bogged down trying to understand exactly *how* the Old Testament meanings of the psalms are connected with the meanings that Jesus draws from them. This is, frankly, a complicated subject. Often, Jesus brings out a level of meaning in the psalms that could not easily have been perceived until he shed his light on them. Furthermore, Jesus does not give lengthy explanations about how the psalms relate to him. Usually, he simply quotes brief fragments of the psalms in the course of discussing various issues with his disciples and his opponents. Keep your attention on *what* Jesus is using the psalm to say about himself, rather than on the complexities of *how* his interpretation of the psalm works.

Second, feel free to focus on whatever level of meaning in each psalm is most relevant to you. The multiple layers of meaning in the psalms are like various floors in a building. My advice is to get off at whatever floor you prefer. If the Old Testament level of meaning in a psalm seems most compelling to you, simply pray the psalm at that level of meaning. In its Old Testament setting, for example, Psalm 8 marvels at God's goodness in creating the human race. If this corresponds to your sentiments, simply pray Psalm 8 as your own statement of wonder and thanks to God. On the other hand, if it is a psalm's connection with Jesus that makes the greatest impression on you, then pray the psalm at that level of meaning. For example, if you find yourself deeply moved by reading Psalm 22 as Jesus' prayer on the cross, pray the psalm as a memorial of his anguish and trust in God.

In exploring the psalms, as in all our exploration of Scripture, a helpful rule is to first take hold of the part you understand and not to worry too much about the parts you do not understand yet.

As we read the psalms, we are not the only searchers. We are looking for Jesus; Jesus is also looking for us.

God sought us before we ever thought of seeking him. The Incarnation—God's Word becoming a human being—was the most awesome phase of God's search for us. The divine Word entered our human world, sharing our joys and sorrows, in order to draw us to God. As God-become-human, Jesus experienced ordinary human life. He took up our prayers of gladness and thanks, of anger and grief, and prayed them as his own. From Nazareth to Jerusalem, he prayed the psalms as one of us.

Having taken on our human nature and experienced our human life, Jesus remains among us, seeking to enter into each of our lives. When we take up the psalms, then, and use them as a means of expressing our joys and sorrows to God, we discover Jesus waiting for us, ready to join us in our praying. When we open the book of Psalms, Jesus *is* here.

Jesus joins us in our prayers to teach us to pray. His most important instruction—an instruction that he gave by example—is to set our hearts on God. Jesus was such a profound interpreter of the psalms because he prayed them with love for the Father, with total willingness to give everything to the Father even when that involved suffering, and with love for other people. As we pray, Jesus will share with us, through the Holy Spirit, his love and his devotion to his Father's will. As we grow in purity of heart, we, like Jesus, will hear God speaking to us in the psalms and will pray them as our wholehearted response.

RULE, MY SON

Questions to Begin

15 minutes
Use a question or two to get warmed up for the reading.

1 Does God have a sense of humor? (If you think so, when have you experienced it?)

2 Describe a situation in which you were mistaken about someone's identity.

5 minutes
Read the passage aloud. Let individuals take turns reading verses of the psalm and paragraphs of the Gospel reading.

The Reading: Psalm 2; Luke 3:15–22

God's Appointed King

Psalm 2:1 Why do the nations conspire,
    and the peoples plot in vain?
2 The kings of the earth set themselves,
    and the rulers take counsel together,
    against the LORD and his anointed, saying,
3 "Let us burst their bonds asunder,
    and cast their cords from us."
4 He who sits in the heavens laughs;
    the LORD has them in derision.
5 Then he will speak to them in his wrath,
    and terrify them in his fury, saying,
6 "I have set my king on Zion, my holy hill."
7 I will tell of the decree of the LORD:
    He said to me, "You are my son;
        today I have begotten you.
8 Ask of me, and I will make the nations your heritage,
    and the ends of the earth your possession.
9 You shall break them with a rod of iron,
    and dash them in pieces like a potter's vessel."
10 Now therefore, O kings, be wise;
    be warned, O rulers of the earth.
11 Serve the LORD with fear,
    with trembling 12 kiss his feet,
    or he will be angry, and you will perish in the way;
        for his wrath is quickly kindled.
    Happy are all who take refuge in him.

Setting the Stage for the Gospel Episode

A prophet named John has spent years praying and fasting in the wilderness of Judea. Now God has instructed him to announce that the time of God's judgment is coming. John goes out to the Jordan River and summons people to turn away from sin and to prepare for the Lord's coming. As a sign of their repentance and readiness for the Lord, John baptizes those who accept his message, immersing them in the water of the Jordan River.

After some time, Jesus arrives at the place where John is baptizing. Jesus also receives John's baptism—perhaps as a sign of his solidarity with sinners. As he prays afterward, God speaks to him, using words from Psalm 2.

The Great King Arrives

Luke 3:15 As the people were filled with expectation, and all were questioning in their hearts concerning John, whether he might be the Messiah, 16 John answered all of them by saying, "I baptize you with water; but one who is more powerful than I is coming; I am not worthy to untie the thong of his sandals. He will baptize you with the Holy Spirit and fire. 17 His winnowing fork is in his hand, to clear his threshing floor and to gather the wheat into his granary; but the chaff he will burn with unquenchable fire."

18 So, with many other exhortations, he proclaimed the good news to the people. . . .

21 Now when all the people were baptized, and when Jesus also had been baptized and was praying, the heaven was opened, 22 and the Holy Spirit descended upon him in bodily form like a dove. And a voice came from heaven, "You are my Son, the Beloved; with you I am well pleased."

10 minutes
Choose questions according to your interest and time.

1 According to Psalm 2, what should the "rulers of the earth" do in order to "serve the Lord with fear" (2:10–11)?

2 How would you describe the emotional tone of Psalm 2? What words or phrases give it this emotional quality?

3 What was good about the "good news" (Luke 3:18) in John's preaching? Was there an element of his message that was not such good news?

4 What is the point of connection between Psalm 2 and the reading from Luke's Gospel?

5 What do the psalm and the Gospel reading communicate about God's relationship with human beings?

A Guide to the Reading

If participants have not read this section already, read it aloud. Otherwise go on to "Questions for Application."

Psalm 2. For centuries, the Israelite people lived as an independent nation, ruled by their own king in Jerusalem. Psalm 2 is a prayer from that age—a fragment from the rituals for enthroning an Israelite king. Its words rang out in the Jerusalem temple as priests, nobles, and common people played their parts in installing and acclaiming the new king.

When the previous king died, the vassal-kings of neighboring countries marshaled their troops for a rebellion (2:1–3). The psalm singer expresses amazement at their ill-advised boldness, for the Israelite king is God's appointee (2:4–6). "His anointed" (2:2) identifies the king as God's representative. During the enthronement ceremony, the king was anointed—smeared with fragrant oil—to show that he was now set apart for royal service to God. In verses 7 through 9 the king himself speaks. Following an ancient custom, he announces that God has given him a prophetic message declaring his adoption on this day of enthronement ("You are my son" was a formula for legalizing an adoption). This ceremony symbolizes that the king is authorized to rule on God's behalf. Thus the king's rule is God's rule. Neighboring kings should take warning (2:10–12)!

The language is poetic. God's "derision" (2:4) and "wrath" (2:5, 12) are metaphors, not literal descriptions. God does not have emotional reactions. God's scorn for enemies figuratively expresses God's total sovereignty and the futility of resistance to his will. Divine anger symbolizes God's unalterable opposition to human sin.

Kingship in Israel eventually came to an end, but the Jewish people continued to pray Psalm 2. It provided an image of God acting vigorously to put down the powers that oppressed them. The psalm nurtured their expectation that God would correct the injustices in the world through a special agent yet to come, an "anointed one"—in Hebrew, a "messiah."

Jesus must have reflected long and hard on this prayer, for it is one of the few psalms that speak explicitly of "the messiah." Jesus' attention may have been drawn especially to verse 7: "I have begotten you." From his earliest days, Jesus knew that he was the Son, uniquely related to God (see Luke 2:49).

Luke 3:15–22. The scene shifts from the temple in Jerusalem to the Jordan river. Jesus is baptized by John the Baptist, a prophet who calls people to repent of their sins. Afterward, as Jesus prays, God speaks to him in the words of Psalm 2: "You are my Son." Talk about Scripture coming alive! God's declaration reveals an incomprehensible mystery: God and the carpenter of Nazareth enjoy a unique relationship of Father and Son.

The quotation of Psalm 2 brings into focus a particular aspect of the baptismal event at the Jordan River: God identifies Jesus as the long-awaited "anointed one"—the Messiah. Standing in the Jordan River, Jesus does not look like the Messiah. He bears no crown or scepter as token of kingship. Yet the words of Psalm 2 proclaim that his baptism is an enthronement. The coming of the Holy Spirit is his anointing (see Luke 4:18–19; Acts 10:37–38). The Messiah has arrived. The time has come for him to put down all human rebellion against God and to establish justice and peace.

But Jesus will not conduct his conquest of sin by crushing all who resist God's will, as Psalm 2:9 might lead us to expect. Rather, Jesus begins his conquest of evil by coming alongside sinners and sharing their baptism of repentance. His ministry will culminate not in destroying his enemies on a battlefield but in asking God to pardon them as he dies on a cross (see Luke 23:34).

In light of God's approaching judgment, John the Baptist called men and women to repent. By submitting to John's baptism, Jesus signals his agreement with John's message. God's judgment is coming; people must prepare. But in the course of his public ministry, Jesus will not emphasize warnings of judgment. Rather, he will stress God's forgiveness (for example, see Luke 15). By his death, Jesus will reconcile sinful men and women with God so that we might be ready to enter God's kingdom when the day of judgment arrives.

Psalm 2 as our prayer. We may now pray Psalm 2 as a celebration of Jesus, the king who conquers the world not with an army but with the power of self-giving love.

Questions for Application

40 minutes
Choose questions according to your interest and time.

1 Reread the last line of Psalm 2. When have you had to take refuge in God? How has this affected your relationship with him?

2 What does it mean to be a son or daughter of God? How do you experience this reality?

3 What has God commissioned *you* to do in the world? How have you experienced the Holy Spirit's help in carrying out your commission? How might you cooperate better with the Spirit's help?

4   Psalm 2 speaks figuratively about God's "fury" and about "trembling" before him (2:5, 11). What kind of fear of God is appropriate? What is inappropriate? (Psalm 34:11–14 and Isaiah 11:1–5 offer food for thought on "fear of the Lord.")

5   The magnitude of evils in the world makes it difficult for some people to believe that God reigns over the world. What enables a person to have faith in God's rule despite the presence of great evils and suffering?

6   For personal reflection: Where in your life does God seem to be calling you to repent of sin? What aspect of this week's readings can spur you or encourage you to take action?

It's everyone's responsibility to make the group work by participating.

Don Cousins and Judson Poling, *Leaders' Guide 1*

Approach to Prayer

15 minutes
Use this approach—or create your own!

◆ Pray Psalm 2 in celebration of Jesus the king who has arrived to overcome the power of sin within us and to show us divine mercy—and pray it also in expectation of the full arrival of his kingdom.

Saints in the Making

You Are My Daughter

This section is a supplement for individual reading.

Vague fears disturbed a woman's quiet life, launching her into a search for God. The turning point of her search came in a conversation with a physician she met when she took her grandson to a Catholic hospital for treatment. The physician was a nun. When the conversation unexpectedly turned to the Bible, the woman described her spiritual confusion. "Why don't you pray *to* the God you are searching for?" the nun asked, and then added, "Talk to him as if he were your friend. . . . Talk to him as if he were your father."

This was a startling idea. The woman came from a culture in which God was revered but would hardly be expected to come down to the level of a personal conversation with a human being. That night, however, as she lay in bed, she remembered her father. No matter how important his work was (he held a high post in the government), he always welcomed interruptions from his little daughter. When he saw her peeking around the door of his office, she recalled, "he would smile and pat the chair next to his. 'Come, my darling, sit here.'" Then, placing his arm around her, he would gently ask what was on her mind. "Suppose God were like a father," the woman suddenly thought. "If my earthly father would put aside everything to listen to me, wouldn't my heavenly Father?" Scrambling out of bed, she knelt on the rug. "My Father . . . ," she prayed.

The woman was Bilquis Sheikh. A Pakistani, she belonged to a wealthy family that traced its lineage back seven centuries. Like most Pakistanis, she was a Muslim. Although she herself was not religious, she was deeply bound to Islam. Her family had supported the local mosque for generations. From her social position, Christianity was a peripheral phenomenon, alien and scorned. Yet her discovery of God as one who reveals himself as Father shook her life to its foundations and opened the way for her to also discover Jesus as the Father's perfect revelation. Her conversion to Christianity, then, disrupted and transformed her entire existence.

For Christians, the concept that God is Father—a concept expressed in God's words to Jesus after his baptism—seems familiar, even trite. The experience of Bilquis Sheikh reminds us of the power of this truth.

The Mouths of Babes

Questions to Begin

15 minutes
Use a question or two to get warmed up for the reading.

1 What's the best way to get noisy children to quiet down?

2 Share a memorable remark by a small child that you have heard—or a remark remembered by your family that you made as a child.

5 minutes
Read the passage aloud. Let individuals take turns reading verses
of the psalm and paragraphs of the Gospel reading.

The Reading: Psalm 8; Matthew 21:8–16

Amazed at God

Psalm 8:1 O LORD, our Sovereign,
how majestic is your name in all the earth!
You have set your glory above the heavens.
2   Out of the mouths of babes and infants
you have founded a bulwark because of your foes,
to silence the enemy and the avenger.
3 When I look at your heavens, the work of your fingers,
the moon and the stars that you have established;
4 what are human beings that you are mindful of them,
mortals that you care for them?
5 Yet you have made them a little lower than God,
and crowned them with glory and honor.
6 You have given them dominion over the works of
your hands;
you have put all things under their feet,
7 all sheep and oxen,
and also the beasts of the field,
8 the birds of the air, and the fish of the sea,
whatever passes along the paths of the seas.
9 O LORD, our Sovereign,
how majestic is your name in all the earth!

Setting the Stage for the Gospel Episode

Our reading now takes us to the last days of Jesus' public ministry.
Jesus is arriving at Jerusalem at Passover time. The city is filled with
pilgrims who have come to celebrate the feast. During his ministry,
Jesus has kept his identity somewhat hidden (see Matthew 8:4;
16:20; 17:9). Now, however, he makes his identity more apparent.
Indeed, he presents himself in a deliberately provocative manner by
riding into Jerusalem on a donkey—a symbolic act by which he
claims to be the king of Israel riding into his capital city in triumph
(see Zechariah 9:9–10). His action positions him as a peaceful and

humble king, rather than one who is warlike and proud (biblical scholar George Montague writes, "He does not choose a chariot but the poorest means of conveyance. Imagine today Jesus entering a modern city not in a limousine but on a bicycle"). Nonetheless, by his ceremonial donkey ride Jesus lays claim to kingship. And as he rides along, the festival crowds welcome him as king.

As soon as Jesus enters the city, he goes to the temple and performs another action symbolizing his authority. This too draws shouts of acclaim from the crowds. When the temple authorities object to the recognition that Jesus is receiving, he quotes Psalm 8 in defense of the crowd.

The King Enters His Capital on a Donkey

Matthew 21:8 A very large crowd spread their cloaks on the road, and others cut branches from the trees and spread them on the road. 9 The crowds that went ahead of him and that followed were shouting,
> "Hosanna to the Son of David!
> Blessed is the one who comes in the name of the Lord!
> Hosanna in the highest heaven!"

10 When he entered Jerusalem, the whole city was in turmoil, asking, "Who is this?" 11 The crowds were saying, "This is the prophet Jesus from Nazareth in Galilee."

12 Then Jesus entered the temple and drove out all who were selling and buying in the temple, and he overturned the tables of the money changers and the seats of those who sold doves. 13 He said to them, "It is written,
> 'My house shall be called a house of prayer';
> but you are making it a den of robbers."

14 The blind and the lame came to him in the temple, and he cured them. 15 But when the chief priests and the scribes saw the amazing things that he did, and heard the children crying out in the temple, "Hosanna to the Son of David," they became angry 16 and said to him, "Do you hear what these are saying?" Jesus said to them, "Yes; have you never read,
> 'Out of the mouths of infants and nursing babies
> you have prepared praise for yourself'?"

10 minutes
Choose questions according to your interest and time.

1 In the psalmist's view, in Psalm 8, what is the most remarkable thing that God has done?

2 In Psalm 8, what are the similarities between God and humans? the differences?

3 The first words of Psalm 8 are repeated at the end of the psalm. How do these words gain meaning through the intervening verses?

4 What is the point of connection between Psalm 8 and the Gospel passage?

5 To whom are the words of Psalm 8:2 addressed? To whom does Jesus refer these words in Matthew 21:16? What does Jesus imply about himself by quoting this part of the psalm?

6 Would Jesus' quotation of Psalm 8 have been likely to persuade those who were displeased that the children were acclaiming him as the Messiah?

A Guide to the Reading

*If participants have not read this section already, read it aloud.
Otherwise go on to "Questions for Application."*

Psalm 8. The psalmist lived before urban lighting turned the night sky a murky gray. In his day, the stars glistened like large diamonds on black velvet. The psalmist gazes in awe at this brilliant array. Yet it is not the heavens but the God who created them that amazes the psalmist. And what he finds most astonishing is not God's great creative power but the great creator's concern for the small and weak and his desire to work through them. God accepts the praise of little ones (8:2). He has placed the frail, mortal human race in a position of honor (8:3–8).

As God's glory shines out in the night sky through the moon and stars, so the divine glory radiates on earth through the human race, which bears a similarity to God (8:5). Psalm 2 celebrated the enthronement of an Israelite king; Psalm 8 sings of the coronation of humanity. God has set our race to govern the earth. Of course, since God is a generous provider, it is assumed that we will likewise exercise our authority over earth's creatures in a benevolent manner (see Genesis 2:15).

I picture a boy looking up at the night sky over Nazareth. Knowing better than anyone else God's love for the human race, young Jesus must have addressed the words of Psalm 8 to God with even greater wonder than the psalmist. Psalm 8 praises God for making humans little less than himself. Now these words were prayed by a human who was not little less than God!

Matthew 21:8–16. The meaning of Jesus' action in the temple is debated. Is he cleansing the temple of inappropriate commercial activity? accusing the temple officials of corruption? indicating that God will destroy the temple and replace it with a more glorious one? symbolizing that the era of the temple is over now that he has come? It is difficult to rule out any of these interpretations. Whatever his intention, Jesus' action asserts his authority to decide what happens with the temple, the central institution of the Jewish people at the time. Like his entry into Jerusalem on a donkey, his action in the temple is a claim to divine authority.

In response, children shout praises. They welcome Jesus as the Messiah. The temple authorities view this as a threat to their authority. But Jesus defends the children with a quotation from Psalm 8:2: "Out of the mouths of infants and nursing babies you have prepared praise for yourself" (Matthew 21:16; because of various translation issues, the quotation in the Gospel diverges from the version of verse 2 given above).

Jesus' quotation of Psalm 8 supports his view that the young, the simple, and the poor are the most likely to perceive God's activity (see Matthew 11:25–27). But it also implies something about himself. Biblical scholar R. T. France writes, "Psalm 8 talks of praise offered to God, not of the acclamation of the Messiah. . . . Is it then only the idea of the acceptability of children's praise to which Jesus refers, or is there implied here a claim to a status even higher than that of 'Son of David'?" By drawing a comparison between the praise of God in Psalm 8 and the children's praise of himself in the temple, Jesus is suggesting that praise to God may rightly be given to him.

Psalm 8 as our prayer. This psalm marvels at the dignity God has bestowed on us as human beings. Looking at Jesus, we can perceive how truly great our dignity is. In Jesus, who is God-become-human, we see that our nature is of such profound dignity that God could take it on himself, becoming one of us and living a human life among us.

The psalmist's amazed question about God's "care" for human beings (8:4) may also be translated, "What are human beings that you *visit* them?" In Jesus, God has indeed made an intimate visit to his human creatures.

Sadly, the marvelous picture of cosmic order in Psalm 8 is marred. Somewhere an "enemy," an "avenger" lurks (8:2). A rebellion against God's order is underway. The human race, delegated by God to rule the world in peace, has sinned; we have not fulfilled our mandate. But now, by Jesus' death, which reconciles us with God, and by the gift of the Spirit, God has restored our capacity to rule the earth justly and peacefully, enabling us to fulfill the role sketched in Psalm 8.

For all this, we can indeed pray Psalm 8 in wonder and thanksgiving!

Questions for Application

40 minutes
Choose questions according to your interest and time.

1   What part does wonder play in
    your relationship with God?
    What can help a person grow in
    wonder at God and his works?

2   When has something wonderful
    given you a sense of God's
    presence and kindness? What
    kind of connections are there
    between God and the goodness
    we experience?

3   Describe a situation in which a
    child was more perceptive than
    adults. In what sense should
    adults seek to be like children
    in their relationship with God?
    In what sense should they not
    imitate children?

4   Identify some attitudes in
    society today that go against
    the view of human dignity
    expressed in Psalm 8. How
    are you influenced by these
    attitudes? How can followers
    of Christ develop an outlook
    on human life that is in keeping
    with the vision of Psalm 8?

5 On a scalke of 1 to 10, how well is the human race carrying out its earthly rule as outlined in Psalm 8? In what ways does Jesus enable us to fulfill this role more effectively?

6 How much of your prayer to God is praise? How might you grow in offering praise to God?

7 Where is God inviting you to grow in humility—to ride a donkey rather than a chariot, a bicycle rather than a limousine?

Interpret objectively what the author has written. . . . Try to discover the thoughts, attitudes, emotions, purpose of the author.

Oletta Wald, *The Joy of Discovery in Bible Study*

Approach to Prayer

15 minutes
Use this approach—or create your own!

◆ Pray Psalm 8 in thanks to
God for all his creatures, for
humankind in particular, and
for visiting us in his Son.

Saints in the Making

Out of the Mouths of Teens

This section is a supplement for individual reading.

M wanga, the king of Buganda, was in a foul mood. He had spent the afternoon hunting hippopotamuses on the lake, but no hippopotamuses were to be found. When he returned to shore, none of his young male attendants were to be seen either. Particularly annoying was the absence of Mwafu, the lad with whom the pedophile king wished to console himself after his frustrating hunt. Informed that the boy was off receiving religious instruction from Sebuggwawo, an older servant, Mwanga flew into a rage. Sebuggwawo was summoned. He admitted he had been instructing Mwafu in Christianity. Grabbing a weapon, Mwanga clubbed Sebuggwawo, then had him dragged off to be killed. The time had come, Mwanga decided, to clear out the rottenness that had invaded his court.

The fuel for this explosion had accumulated for some time. In the 1880s, English and German colonizers were probing the borders of Mwanga's territory (in present-day Uganda). Anglican and Catholic missionaries were gaining converts—and the converts quickly demonstrated that their first loyalty was to their new God (and their second was perhaps to their new European friends), rather than to the king.

The day after the incident with Sebuggwawo, Mwanga assembled his retinue of officials and the young men and boys who served as his pages. About thirty pages identified themselves as Christians. Mwanga handed them over to the executioners. Many were teenagers. Three of them—Mugagga, Mbaga-Tuzinde, and Gyavira—were about sixteen years old. The youngest, Kizito, was only thirteen. Despite their youth, they faced death bravely, telling their executioners, in the classic declaration of Christian martyrs, "You can destroy our bodies, but not our souls." One writer records that "they were as merry as if they were going for a holiday." The young men and boys were burned to death on June 3, 1886. Describing the final scene, another author writes: "They continued to reassure each other and awaited death singing the hymns of the religion for which they were being executed." Jesus' words would make a fitting epitaph: "Out of the mouths of infants and nursing babies you have prepared praise for yourself" (Matthew 21:16).

This Was to Be Expected

Questions to Begin

15 minutes
Use a question or two to get warmed up for the reading.

1 What was your least happy experience of renting something or renting something out?

2 When have you gone away from home and been surprised by what you discovered when you returned?

5 minutes
Read the passage aloud. Suggestion: Designate one participant to
read verses 5–19, 21, and 28; let the rest of the group read the
other verses in unison.

The Reading: Psalm 118:5–29; Matthew 21:33–43

A Psalm of Thanks

^{Psalm 118:5} Out of my distress I called on the LORD;
    the LORD answered me and set me in a broad
        place. . . .
  ¹⁰ All nations surrounded me;
    in the name of the LORD I cut them off!
  ¹¹ They surrounded me, surrounded me on every side;
    in the name of the LORD I cut them off! . . .
  ¹³ I was pushed hard, so that I was falling,
    but the LORD helped me.
  ¹⁴ The LORD is my strength and my might;
    he has become my salvation. . . .
  ¹⁷ I shall not die, but I shall live,
    and recount the deeds of the LORD.
  ¹⁸ The LORD has punished me severely,
    but he did not give me over to death.
  ¹⁹ Open to me the gates of righteousness,
    that I may enter through them
    and give thanks to the LORD.
  ²⁰ This is the gate of the LORD;
    the righteous shall enter through it.
  ²¹ I thank you that you have answered me
    and have become my salvation.
  ²² The stone that the builders rejected
    has become the chief cornerstone.
  ²³ This is the LORD's doing;
    it is marvelous in our eyes.
  ²⁴ This is the day that the LORD has made;
    let us rejoice and be glad in it.
  ²⁵ Save us, we beseech you, O LORD!
    O LORD, we beseech you, give us success!
  ²⁶ Blessed is the one who comes in the name of the LORD.
    We bless you from the house of the LORD. . . .
  ²⁸ You are my God, and I will give thanks to you;
    you are my God, I will extol you.
  ²⁹ O give thanks to the LORD for he is good,
    for his steadfast love endures forever.

Setting the Stage for the Gospel Episode

In Jerusalem, in the final days of his ministry, Jesus teaches in the temple day after day, which brings him into conflict with the officials who administer the temple and with other religious experts. Jesus uses a parable to show what he thinks of their opposition to him—and to give a hint of his identity as God's Son. He drives his point home with a quotation from Psalm 118.

Jesus Tells a Story

Matthew 21:33 "There was a landowner who planted a vineyard, put a fence around it, dug a wine press in it, and built a watchtower. Then he leased it to tenants and went to another country. 34 When the harvest time had come, he sent his slaves to the tenants to collect his produce. 35 But the tenants seized his slaves and beat one, killed another, and stoned another. 36 Again he sent other slaves, more than the first; and they treated them in the same way. 37 Finally he sent his son to them, saying, 'They will respect my son.' 38 But when the tenants saw the son, they said to themselves, 'This is the heir; come, let us kill him and get his inheritance.' 39 So they seized him, threw him out of the vineyard, and killed him. 40 Now when the owner of the vineyard comes, what will he do to those tenants?" 41 They said to him, "He will put those wretches to a miserable death, and lease the vineyard to other tenants who will give him the produce at the harvest time."
42 Jesus said to them, "Have you never read in the scriptures:
'The stone that the builders rejected
has become the cornerstone;
this was the Lord's doing,
and it is amazing in our eyes'?
43 Therefore I tell you, the kingdom of God will be taken away from you and given to a people that produces the fruits of the kingdom."

10 minutes
Choose questions according to your interest and time.

1 Psalm 118 is an expression of thanks. Who is giving thanks? For what are the psalmist and others thanking God?

2 What indications can you find that Psalm 118 was designed for some kind of liturgical celebration?

3 What is the point of connection between Psalm 118 and the Gospel passage?

4 In Jesus' parable, whom does the landowner represent? the son? Whom do the tenants represent? You may find it helpful to refer to the context in Matthew's Gospel (Matthew 21:23–32).

5 Does Jesus seem surprised by the rejection he has encountered from the religious leaders? Why?

6 Judging from the parable he tells, what does Jesus expect is going to happen to him?

A Guide to the Reading

If participants have not read this section already, read it aloud. Otherwise go on to "Questions for Application."

Psalm 118. With this psalm we return to the temple in Jerusalem. The city and temple are crowded with people apparently celebrating a military success. The king enters the city in a parade, proclaiming the victory God has given him. As he arrives at the temple, Psalm 118 provides the text for an exchange of greetings and acclamations. The king asks permission to enter the temple gate and give thanks to God. The priests welcome him into the temple courtyard. King, priests, and people then rejoice in God's protection. The king speaks verses 5–7, 10–14, 17–19, 21, and 28; priests and people speak the rest.

The king is elated. He was in difficult straits, but God rescued him. Verse 17 may be translated: "I did not die but lived!" The crowd expresses amazement at the way God reversed their sagging fortunes. Israel was small and powerless, their king close to defeat (118:10–13). They seemed as useless as a flawed stone abandoned by stonemasons. But this stone was suddenly picked up and used as the most important stone of the building (118:22–23)! Seemingly insignificant Israel and its not-very-impressive king were shown to have a crucial role in God's plans.

The Jews continued to pray Psalm 118 long after they stopped having a king. It expressed their longing for God to send a king to fight for them, give them justice, and lead them in thanking God. In the meantime, however, in the centuries before the birth of Jesus, the Jews were a small and politically weak people, a stone disregarded by the builders of empires.

As a young man visiting Jerusalem for the festivals, Jesus must often have entered the temple singing Psalm 118 with the crowds of people. As the worshipers flowed up the immense staircases and ramps into the huge temple plaza, chanting the psalm, they had no idea that the king, the "cornerstone," was already among them!

Matthew 21:33–44. In the course of his ministry, some people accepted Jesus, but by and large, the religious leaders did not. Jesus now tells a parable that shows how he views this situation.

Those who listened to Jesus' parable would have understood that the landowner represented God. By comparing himself to the landowner's son, Jesus implicitly claims to be God's Son. The parable also implies that the Jewish leaders will no longer play a central role in pastoring God's people (see Matthew 21:41, 43). At the end of the parable, Jesus applies to himself the statement in Psalm 118:22–23 about the rejected stone. Thus he indicates that he is the king whom Jews have been expecting when they prayed this psalm. He also indicates that the religious leaders' rejection of him is no surprise. It was foreshadowed long ago in Psalm 118.

We can easily understand why Jesus' quotation of Psalm 118:22–23 was remembered by his early followers after his death and resurrection. Their fellow Jews challenged them with a difficult question: "How can you claim that Jesus is the Messiah promised by God when the leaders of the Jewish people did not accept him as such?" Their answer, which the early Christians drew from Psalm 118:22–23, was that the rejection of the Messiah fell into a familiar pattern. Often in the past, people had refused to listen to those whom God sent to instruct or lead them. Often the stone had been rejected by the builders. The religious leaders who rejected Jesus played into this unhappy pattern. Their failure to recognize the Messiah was to have been expected.

Psalm 118 as our prayer. In light of the resurrection of Jesus, this psalm is more than ever a prayer of thanksgiving for a victory granted by God—the victory that Jesus achieved through God's power, the victory of his resurrection (see Acts 4:11; 1 Peter 2:7). In the psalm, the Israelite king rejoices because God has saved him from being killed in battle (118:17). As the prayer of Jesus the king, these words declare not his rescue *from* death but his triumph *over* it. The Israelite king celebrated a military victory that was good news for the whole nation. Now Psalm 118 celebrates a victory that is not for the benefit of Jesus alone but is for all humanity, for Jesus has died and risen as the representative of us all. Verse 21 celebrates his resurrection and entry into heaven. There, as our risen representative, he leads us in praising God. Truly, the day of the Lord's making, the day of rejoicing for all of us (118:24), is the day when Jesus rose from the dead.

Questions for Application

40 minutes
Choose questions according to your interest and time.

1 When has something wonderful given you a sense of God's presence and kindness?

2 What situations in your past could be summed up by Psalm 118:5? Do you continue to thank God for his help?

3 Where in your life do you need a power greater than your own? How do you ask God for his help? How could you grow in seeking God's help in this situation?

4 Do you ever tell other people about the ways in which you have experienced God's help? How might you do this more?

5 What fruit is God hoping to get from you today? this week? in this period of your life?

6 Jesus' quotation of Psalm 118 leads us to reflect on our tendency not to recognize God's initiatives in our lives. Looking back, what situation in your life seems to have contained some invitation from God that you did not notice at the time? What might you learn from this experience?

7 How might your reflection on Psalm 118 deepen your participation in the celebration of the Eucharist?

You don't have to become an expert on the Bible, but you do need to become a more competent reader.

Steve Mueller, *The Seeker's Guide to Reading the Bible*

Approach to Prayer

15 minutes
Use this approach—or create your own!

◆ Ask someone to read aloud the account of Jesus' resurrection in Matthew 28:1–10. Then pray the portion of Psalm 118 on page 31 in celebration of his resurrection. Close with a Glory to the Father.

A Living Tradition

Hosanna?

This section is a supplement for individual reading.

There is a connection between our psalm this week and last week's Gospel reading, but it is not easy to see. Psalm 118:25–26 reads: "Save us, we beseech you, O Lord! O Lord, we beseech you, give us success! Blessed is the one who comes in the name of the Lord." Over centuries before the time of Jesus, the Hebrew words that are translated "Save us, we beseech you!" became a standard formula, like other Hebrew phrases, such as "Amen" ("Surely!") and "Alleluia" ("Praise the Lord!"). For this reason, perhaps, Matthew did not translate the phrase into Greek in his account of Jesus' triumphal entry into Jerusalem. Matthew tells us that "the crowds that went ahead of him and that followed were shouting, 'Hosanna to the Son of David! Blessed is the one who comes in the name of the Lord!'" (21:9). "Hosanna" reflects the Hebrew for "Save us, we beseech you!"

Once we see the connection between Psalm 118 and Matthew 21, it is easy to recognize the connection between Psalm 118 and the Mass. In the Mass, we sing, "Holy, holy, holy, Lord God of power and might. Heaven and earth are full of your glory. Hosanna in the highest! Blessed is he who comes in the name of the Lord. Hosanna in the highest!" The first section comes from Isaiah 6:3; the section beginning with "Hosanna" comes from Psalm 118, via Matthew 21.

Knowing the origin of the acclamation helps us understand its meaning in the Mass. In ancient days, Jews used Psalm 118 to hail a conquering king coming to the temple to give thanks for a victory. The crowd on Palm Sunday took up the chant from Psalm 118 to acknowledge Jesus as the greatest conquering king, the Messiah, who had conducted a victorious ministry against the powers of sickness and sin and who was now coming to carry out God's greatest act of liberation. These meanings flow into our use of "Hosanna" in the Mass. In the Mass, we sing "Hosanna" as we are beginning to recall Jesus' final meal with his disciples and his death and resurrection. Thus we are acclaiming Jesus as the great king who has come to save us from our sins and from death's power—and who is now coming to renew his kingdom in us through Holy Communion.

SOMEONE GREATER THAN YOU THINK

Questions to Begin

15 minutes
Use a question or two to get warmed up for the reading.

---

1 When have you discovered that a person you met was much more notable than you realized at first?

---

2 Describe a debate or argument in which someone (perhaps you) suddenly turned the tables on the other person.

5 minutes
Read the passage aloud. Let individuals take turns reading verses
of the psalm and paragraphs of the Gospel reading.

The Reading: Psalm 110:1–5; Matthew 22:41–46; 26:59–66

Assurances for a King

Psalm 110:1 The LORD says to my lord,
"Sit at my right hand
until I make your enemies your footstool."
2 The LORD sends out from Zion
your mighty scepter.
Rule in the midst of your foes.
3 Your people will offer themselves willingly
on the day you lead your forces
on the holy mountains.
From the womb of the morning,
like dew, your youth will come to you.
4 The LORD has sworn and will not change his mind,
"You are a priest forever according to the order of
Melchizedek."
5 The Lord is at your right hand;
he will shatter kings on the day of his wrath.

Setting the Stage for the Gospel Episode (1)

Jesus continues to teach in the temple and debate with those who do not accept his teaching. Finally, he challenges his opponents to solve a problem concerning the interpretation of Psalm 110. Their failure to do so puts an end to their arguments with him.

Stumping the Experts

Matthew 22:41 Now while the Pharisees were gathered together, Jesus asked them this question: 42 "What do you think of the Messiah? Whose son is he?" They said to him, "The son of David." 43 He said to them, "How is it then that David by the Spirit calls him Lord, saying,
44 'The Lord said to my Lord,
"Sit at my right hand,
until I put your enemies under your feet"'?

45 If David thus calls him Lord, how can he be his son?" 46 No one was able to give him an answer, nor from that day did anyone dare to ask him any more questions.

Setting the Stage for the Gospel Episode (2)

After the religious authorities stop challenging Jesus in public, they devise a plan to have him put to death. A day or two after the preceding exchange in the temple, the religious authorities arrest Jesus. Gathering at night, the men who govern the temple interrogate Jesus about his teaching and activities. Finally, they challenge him to declare openly whether he claims to be the Messiah. In response, Jesus affirms his identity and expresses his privileged relationship with God with an allusion to Psalm 110.

A Courageous Decision

Matthew 26:59 Now the chief priests and the whole council were looking for false testimony against Jesus so that they might put him to death, 60 but they found none, though many false witnesses came forward. At last two came forward 61 and said, "This fellow said, 'I am able to destroy the temple of God and to build it in three days.'" 62 The high priest stood up and said, "Have you no answer? What is it that they testify against you?" 63 But Jesus was silent. Then the high priest said to him, "I put you under oath before the living God, tell us if you are the Messiah, the Son of God." 64 Jesus said to him, "You have said so. But I tell you,

> From now on you will see the Son of Man
>> seated at the right hand of Power
>> and coming on the clouds of heaven."

65 Then the high priest tore his clothes and said, "He has blasphemed! Why do we still need witnesses? You have now heard his blasphemy. 66 What is your verdict?" They answered, "He deserves death."

Questions for Careful Reading

10 minutes
Choose questions according to your interest and time.

1	Identify two points of similarity between Psalm 110 and Psalm 2. Identify two points of similarity between Psalm 110 and Psalm 118.
2	What are the points of connection between Psalm 110 and the Gospel passages?
3	In the discussion of Psalm 110 by Jesus and the religious experts, who is assumed to have written this psalm?
4	What assumption about fathers and sons lies behind Jesus' question in Matthew 22:45?
5	It is unlikely that Jesus means to imply that the Messiah will *not* be David's son. What other possible ways might there be to answer his questions to the Pharisees in Matthew 22?

A Guide to the Reading

If participants have not read this section already, read it aloud. Otherwise go on to "Questions for Application."

Psalm 110. Psalm 110 is not an easy prayer to understand—or to pray. The meaning of the Hebrew is so unclear that parts of it are impossible to translate with certainty. Yet the psalm is worth our investigating, since Jesus made such prominent use of it. His quotation of Psalm 110 in the temple resounds as the final word of his public ministry.

Like Psalm 118, Psalm 110 may have been written to celebrate an Israelite king's military victory. The verbs in verses 5 and 6 may be translated in the past tense: the Lord has *already* fought on behalf of the king. On the other hand, this psalm, like Psalm 2, may reflect the ceremony for enthroning a new king. As in Psalm 2, here also there is a prophetic declaration to the king—in fact, two declarations (110:1, 4; compare Psalm 2:7–9).

Matthew 22:41–46. In Jesus' time, people considered David to have been the author of this psalm—a viewpoint Jesus accepts (modern scholars think the psalm may indeed go back to the time of David, a thousand years before Jesus). People interpreted the psalm as predicting a great future king—the Messiah. In this interpretation, God tells the Messiah, "Sit on your throne and rule, for I have appointed you priest-king."

Since David was held to be the speaker of the psalm and the Messiah was held to be a descendant of David, it seemed that in verse 1 David is speaking of his own descendant as his "lord." That, however, ran contrary to ancient thinking, which regarded fathers as greater than their sons. This was a puzzle, and much to their embarrassment, the religious leaders admit they cannot explain it. Jesus does not explain it either, but he leaves the impression that the Messiah *is* somehow greater than David. The Messiah is David's "son"—but also God's Son. Having supernatural status, the Messiah will bring a kingdom greater than David's political regime.

Jesus' use of Psalm 110 gives us an insight into his character. The psalm speaks of a king who rules over his enemies by the usual means, that is, through military conquest. Jesus read the psalm as addressed to himself; he saw himself as God's appointed ruler. Yet he discerned that his path to conquest lay not through force of arms but through the relinquishment of earthly goods, including his life. How finely attuned to God's purposes Jesus was, to interpret this psalm of empowerment in a way that ran contrary to common expectations—and contrary to his own natural human reluctance to die.

Matthew 26:59–66. Dragged before the council of officials who run the Jerusalem temple, Jesus appears to be powerless, discredited, abandoned by God. Nevertheless, he boldly applies to himself the image of sitting at the right hand of God from Psalm 110:1. This is a powerful way of declaring that God will vindicate him. Nothing more clearly illustrates Jesus' unshakable conviction of his identity as God's representative to the human race than his assertion that he will be seen sitting at God's right hand, that is, ruling with God. His seemingly hopeless condition could not shake his confidence in his unique relationship with God and his destined sharing in God's reign.

Psalm 110 as our prayer. The early Christians made such heavy use of Psalm 110 that it became the most widely quoted psalm in the New Testament. The John who wrote the book of Revelation, for example, employs the image of Jesus sitting down next to God and speaks of Jesus inviting us to sit beside him (see Revelation 3:21). This image of our sharing in Jesus' divine rule is a figurative way of declaring that we will share in his victory over death, since it is over death, above all, that we will be conquerors with him.

Since Jesus used Psalm 110:1 to express his certainty that God would vindicate him, this verse now reminds us that all who follow him will also be vindicated by God. Vindication is not a concept to which most of us give much attention. Yet it is worth our reflection. God will ultimately demonstrate that all those who seemed weak or foolish for following Jesus on the path of humble service were actually walking on the royal road of his kingdom. Small acts of love that seemed like insignificant wastes of time will be shown to have been of great importance to God (see Matthew 10:42; 25:31–40).

Thus Psalm 110 both reminds us of Jesus' lordship and celebrates our hope in him.

Questions for Application

40 minutes
Choose questions according to your interest and time.

1 Jesus' question about Psalm 110 makes the point that his kingdom is greater than people expect. When has God's greatness or love surprised you? How has this experience affected your life?

2 In what ways is Jesus' reign felt in the world today? Why are signs of God's kingdom sometimes difficult to detect?

3 Recall a situation in which you found it difficult to affirm your faith in God. What have you found to be helpful for sustaining your faith in situations of this kind?

4 At his trial, Jesus looked powerless, yet he asserted the truth of his sharing in God's rule. Identify a situation today in which God's reign seems weak or insignificant. How can a person grow in the capacity of measuring the world according to God's scale of values?

5 When has the hope of eternal life with God been especially important to you? What effect does it have on your ordinary life?

6 For personal reflection: What small, secret act of kindness could you perform for someone this week as an expression of your faith that in God's kingdom no act of love is unimportant?

Recommended guideline for Bible discussion groups: "We will talk about ourselves and our own situations, avoiding conversation about other people."

Christian Basics Bible Studies

Approach to Prayer

15 minutes
Use this approach—or create your own!

◆ Pray Psalm 110:1–3 together.
Then take time for individuals
to mention the needs of people
they know or know of. After
each need, pray together the
petition from the Our Father:
"Your kingdom come, your will
be done, on earth as it is in
heaven." At the end of all the
petitions, pray the entire Our
Father together, looking
forward to the complete
coming of God's kingdom.

A Living Tradition

Receive Our Prayer!

This section is a supplement for individual reading.

At his trial, Jesus drew on the first verse of Psalm 110 to express his confidence that God would vindicate him. This verse speaks of a king of Israel being enthroned next to God's throne—an image that conveys the message that the king is authorized to rule on God's behalf. Jesus' allusion to this verse in his declaration to those who had arrested him—"You will see the Son of Man seated at the right hand of Power" (Matthew 26:64)—was a way of saying, "You see me now tied up and powerless, hardly looking like the Messiah. But make no mistake, I am indeed the one whom God has authorized to save his people. In the future, you will see that I share in God's rule over humanity."

The image of a king seated next to God's throne is rich in meaning. It symbolizes not only sharing in God's authority but also playing an intercessory role with God. Being seated next to God suggests intimacy with God (see Hebrews 1:13). A human who was seated next to God would be in a position to be the perfect intermediary between God and human beings. This dimension of the seated-next-to-God image is taken up in the letter to the Hebrews (Hebrews 8:1). It is also employed in the Mass.

On Sundays and feast days, the opening section of the Mass includes a song of praise called the "Gloria," because it begins "Glory to God in the highest." After honoring the Father, the "Gloria" moves on to praise the Son. Jesus is addressed with these words: "You who are seated at the right hand of the Father, receive our prayer." The prayer pictures Jesus enthroned beside the Father, not only ruling with him as God but also interceding with him as God-made-human. Just as we end many prayers by asking God to accept our requests "through Jesus Christ, our Lord," so in the "Gloria" we ask Jesus to receive our requests and to deliver them to his Father. Because Jesus is a human being like us, we can be sure that he understands our needs; because he is one with the Father, seated next to God, we can be sure that any prayer conveyed by him will receive a favorable hearing.

SUFFERING MUST PLAY A PART

Questions to Begin

15 minutes
Use a question or two to get warmed up for the reading.

1 When has someone come to your aid when others were making fun of you? When have you done the same for someone else?

2 When have you been falsely accused of something? What was this experience like for you?

5 minutes
Read the passages aloud. Let individuals take turns reading
sections of the psalm and paragraphs of the Gospel reading.

The Reading: Psalm 69:1–33; John 15:19–25

Desperate Straits

Psalm 69:1 Save me, O God,
  for the waters have come up to my neck.
2 I sink in deep mire,
  where there is no foothold;
I have come into deep waters,
  and the flood sweeps over me.
3 I am weary with my crying;
  my throat is parched.
My eyes grow dim
  with waiting for my God.
4 More in number than the hairs of my head
  are those who hate me without cause;
many are those who would destroy me,
  my enemies who accuse me falsely.
What I did not steal
  must I now restore?
5 O God, you know my folly;
  the wrongs I have done are not hidden from you.
6 Do not let those who hope in you be put to shame
    because of me,
  O Lord GOD of hosts;
do not let those who seek you be dishonored because
    of me,
  O God of Israel.
7 It is for your sake that I have borne reproach,
  that shame has covered my face. . . .
9 It is zeal for your house that has consumed me;
  the insults of those who insult you have fallen
    on me. . . .
16 Answer me, O LORD, for your steadfast love is good;
  according to your abundant mercy, turn to me.
17 Do not hide your face from your servant,
  for I am in distress—make haste to answer me. . . .

^{20} Insults have broken my heart,
  so that I am in despair.
 I looked for pity, but there was none;
  and for comforters, but I found none.
^{21} They gave me poison for food,
  and for my thirst they gave me vinegar to drink. . . .
^{29} I am lowly and in pain;
  let your salvation, O God, protect me.
^{30} I will praise the name of God with a song;
  I will magnify him with thanksgiving. . . .
^{32} Let the oppressed see it and be glad;
  you who seek God, let your hearts revive.
^{33} For the LORD hears the needy,
  and does not despise his own that are in bonds.

Setting the Stage for the Gospel Episode

Our Gospel reading takes us back a few hours before last week's reading about Jesus' interrogation (Matthew 26:59–66). In this reading, Jesus is eating his final meal with his followers before his arrest. In the course of the meal, Jesus warns them that they will meet with the same kind of opposition that he has encountered. In his reflections on the hostility that has been directed at him, Jesus quotes Psalm 69:4 (differences in translations make it a little difficult to recognize the quotation).

Jesus' Warning to His Disciples

John 15:19 "If you belonged to the world, the world would love you as its own. Because you do not belong to the world, but I have chosen you out of the world—therefore the world hates you. ^{20} Remember the word that I said to you, 'Servants are not greater than their master.' If they persecuted me, they will persecute you; if they kept my word, they will keep yours also. . . . ^{24} If I had not done among them the works that no one else did, they would not have sin. But now they have seen and hated both me and my Father. ^{25} It was to fulfill the word that is written in their law, 'They hated me without a cause.'"

10 minutes
Choose questions according to your interest and time.

1 Which statements in the psalm seem to be literal descriptions of the psalmist's situation? Which statements seem metaphorical?

2 In Psalm 69, what is the difference between the section that runs from verse 1 through verse 29 and the section from verse 30 through verse 32? How would you account for the sudden shift between verse 29 and verse 30?

3 What is the point of connection between Psalm 69 and the Gospel passage?

4 What does Jesus mean by the term "the world" in John 15:19?

5 What view of personal responsibility for sin does Jesus express in John 15:24?

6 In John 15:25, Jesus identifies himself as someone who could pray Psalm 69 as his own prayer. What portions of the psalm seem especially fitting for him? Are there parts that do not seem suitable for him?

A Guide to the Reading

If participants have not read this section already, read it aloud. Otherwise go on to "Questions for Application."

Psalm 69. Up to this week, our psalms have been public prayers. Three were prayers for ceremonies in the temple (Psalms 2, 118, 110). Psalm 8 was a grand public prayer, with the whole human race in view. By contrast, Psalm 69 brings us inside one person's inner experience. And while our earlier psalms celebrated God's actions, Psalm 69 decries God's inaction. From praise and thanks, we shift here to a darker mood. A person surrounded by enemies and laid low by sickness cries out to God, who is not providing any relief. Scholar Mitchell Dahood points out that despite the fact that the psalmist is almost drowning in floodwaters, the psalmist's throat is dry and hoarse from crying to God for help (69:3). The psalmist's eyesight is failing from the strain of looking in vain for God's intervention (69:3).

The psalmist is suffering both human animosity and bodily illness—a frequent combination in psalms of distress (for example, Psalms 6; 13; 22; 31; 35; 38; 71; 88). Possibly the psalmist's hostile neighbors interpret his or her illness as a sign of guilt and divine punishment. This was the outlook of Job's so-called comforters (although God declared they were mistaken—Job 42:7). The psalmist acknowledges having sinned (Psalm 69:5), but denies the serious allegations that hostile neighbors are making (69:4). In fact, the psalmist is suffering for God's cause (69:7, 9).

Growing up, Jesus may often have heard Psalm 69 prayed by people in distress—neighbors, friends, family. In first-century Galilee, mishaps, diseases, and political exploitation meant that the miseries of ill health and injustice were never far away. There was no effective medical care and no judicial system where a poor person could secure justice. As Jesus heard this psalm prayed and prayed it himself, he may have become increasingly aware that it foreshadowed his own persecution and physical suffering. Did he recoil at the prospect of pain and rejection that lay before him, as he later did in Gethsemane (see Mark 14:32–42)?

John 15:19–25. Some of Jesus' fellow Jews expected the Messiah to be a powerful military leader, since they looked for him to break the forces of oppression and injustice in the world. They hoped for a king who would vanquish the Roman overlords, then lead God's people into holiness and bring about more glorious worship in the temple. Jesus accepted the idea of a kingly Messiah, but he worked a double transformation in the concept. First, he made it more spiritual: he would not achieve a military and political victory over men and women who opposed God's will; rather, he would triumph in a spiritual way over the powers of sin and death. Second, he would conquer not by an exercise of power but by love working through his own weakness and suffering.

In effect, Jesus combined the idea of a kingly Messiah with another Jewish idea—the notion that the suffering of those who are faithful to God may be an instrument of God's action in the world. This idea is expressed, for example, in Isaiah 52:13–53:12. We can see it also in psalms such as Psalm 69, in which a just person suffers deeply and looks forward to being rescued by God in a way that will bring blessings and joy to other people. No one before Jesus, it seems, had connected these two strands of Jewish thought; no one had entertained the possibility of a *suffering* Messiah.

At the Last Supper, Jesus quotes only a single line from Psalm 69. But for those familiar with it, as his disciples would have been, that line would bring the whole psalm to mind. By connecting verse 4 with himself, Jesus implies that the rest of the psalm also speaks about him. On another occasion, Jesus showed his followers that it was written "in the law of Moses, the prophets, and the psalms" that the Messiah was to suffer and rise from the dead (see Luke 24:44–45). Psalm 69 may well be one of those psalms by which Jesus explained that it was through his suffering that reconciliation with God and life in the Spirit would come to men and women.

Psalm 69 as our prayer. We may pray this psalm as a memorial of Jesus' willingness to go the way of suffering and death in order to bring us into life with God (see page 59). Remembering that Jesus prayed Psalm 69 in the face of his suffering may strengthen our trust in God when we use it as our prayer in times of difficulty and grief.

Questions for Application

40 minutes
Choose questions according to your interest and time.

1 What various means do people use to get God to help them when they are in distress? What means does the psalmist use in Psalm 69? Are there appropriate and inappropriate ways of trying to obtain God's help?

2 When have you seen God's help or blessing for one person have a positive effect on other people?

3 Are there helpful and unhelpful ways of communicating to other people our experience of God's help and blessings?

4 Why are Christians sometimes disliked? Which reasons have to do with Christians' faithfulness to Christ? Which have to do with Christians' failure to faithfully reflect their master?

5 Where in your life does others' lack of encouragement or approval, or even their opposition, hold you back from doing what you think God wishes you to do? How might you act differently if you cared more about God's approval and less about other people's?

6 Briefly describe someone you know who chose to accept some disadvantage or loss in order to do what they thought God was calling them to do. What can you learn from their experience?

7 By making Psalm 69 his own prayer, Jesus expressed solidarity with everyone who suffers injustice (69:4). How can you grow in expressing solidarity with those who experience injustice?

Dear brethren, we exhort you to acquire a loving familiarity with the written word. . . . This intimate knowledge of Holy Writ will bring you close to the person and life of our Savior and to the labors of his apostles. It will renew in your hearts the joy with which the first Christians received the tidings of salvation.

National Conference of Catholic Bishops, 1919

Approach to Prayer

15 minutes
Use this approach—or create your own!

◆ Ask someone to read aloud the passage from John's Gospel (page 52). Take time for silent reflection. Then pray the following prayer together.

Lord Jesus,
You are the way to the Father;
you alone have the words of
    eternal life.
Help me to be faithful to you,
to follow you closely,
even when that means having to
    endure
misunderstanding and
    opposition.
Help me to reflect your kindness,
your humility,
your willingness to serve,
even in service of those who do
    not support me
in following you.
Lord, lead men and women
    everywhere
to yourself.

A Living Tradition

The Sufferings of Christ

This section is a supplement for individual reading.

Jesus interpreted Psalm 69 as a prophecy of his sufferings. On this basis, St. Robert Bellarmine, a sixteenth-century Italian theologian, believed the psalm to be a source of insights into Jesus' experience of suffering—insights that complement the portrait of Jesus that we find in the Gospels. Unlike the psalmist, who was weary with crying out to God (69:3), in the Gospels Jesus is almost entirely silent in his suffering. His silence, Bellarmine writes, was due not to the mildness of his suffering but to the greatness of his perseverance. If Jesus' outcry in his suffering had corresponded to the intensity of his pain, Bellarmine writes, Jesus' throat would have been as dry as the psalmist's with shouting for help, and his eyes would have been as strained with looking for divine assistance. In Bellarmine's view, "The prophet expressed the magnitude of Jesus' suffering, while the Gospel writers expressed the greatness of his steadiness, his firmness of character." Here are a couple of Bellarmine's comments on Psalm 69.

69:1–2. This image of waters up to his neck refers to the many torments that Christ endured, for he did not simply die but bore countless pains and sorrows. The "deep mire" into which he is stuck signifies the sins of the whole human race, which held him down. The "flood" that sweeps over him is the divine decree that wills him to remove sins by his suffering and death. The flood may also be understood to refer to the cruelty of those who put him to death—and also, and most especially, to his own tremendous love for humankind.

69:20. In such great suffering, Jesus had no one to console him. While there were some who suffered with Christ as he died, no one was saddened for the reasons that he was sad. The apostles and the pious women were sorrowful on account of Christ's physical death, but he himself was sorrowful on account of a spiritual death—the spiritual blindness of those who rejected him, who raged against the physician who had come to heal them. In his agony, Christ sought consolation but did not find it: the consolation he sought was the conversion of sinners, but during his agony, hardly anyone was converted. Admittedly, there was the thief (Luke 23:39–43), but he was converted only at the end.

Why Have You Forsaken Me?

Questions to Begin

15 minutes
Use a question or two to get warmed up for the reading.

---

1   When have you been frightened by an animal?

2   When have you responded to a cry for help?

Opening the Bible

5 minutes
Read the passages aloud. Let individuals take turns reading
sections of the psalm and paragraphs of the Gospel reading.

The Reading: Mark 15:24–37; Psalm 22:1–31

The Death of Jesus

Mark 15:24 And they crucified him, and divided his clothes among
them, casting lots to decide what each should take.

25 It was nine o'clock in the morning when they crucified
him. . . .

34 At three o'clock Jesus cried out with a loud voice, "Eloi,
Eloi, lema sabachthani?" which means, "My God, my God, why have
you forsaken me?" 35 When some of the bystanders heard it, they
said, "Listen, he is calling for Elijah." 36 And someone ran, filled a
sponge with sour wine, put it on a stick, and gave it to him to drink,
saying, "Wait, let us see whether Elijah will come to take him down."
37 Then Jesus gave a loud cry and breathed his last.

The Prayer Jesus Began to Pray

Psalm 22:1 My God, my God, why have you forsaken me?
  Why are you so far from helping me, from the
   words of my groaning?
 2 O my God, I cry by day, but you do not answer;
  and by night, but find no rest. . . .
 6 But I am a worm, and not human;
  scorned by others, and despised by the people.
 7 All who see me mock at me;
  they make mouths at me, they shake their heads;
 8 "Commit your cause to the LORD; let him deliver—
  let him rescue the one in whom he delights!"
 9 Yet it was you who took me from the womb;
  you kept me safe on my mother's breast.
 10 On you I was cast from my birth,
  and since my mother bore me you have been my God.
 11 Do not be far from me,
  for trouble is near
  and there is no one to help. . . .
 14 I am poured out like water,
  and all my bones are out of joint;

my heart is like wax;
      it is melted within my breast;
15 my mouth is dried up like a potsherd,
      and my tongue sticks to my jaws;
    you lay me in the dust of death.
16 For dogs are all around me;
      a company of evildoers encircles me.
  My hands and feet have shriveled;
17 I can count all my bones.
  They stare and gloat over me;
18 they divide my clothes among themselves,
      and for my clothing they cast lots.
19 But you, O Lord, do not be far away!
    O my help, come quickly to my aid!
20 Deliver my soul from the sword,
      my life from the power of the dog!
        21Save me from the mouth of the lion!
  From the horns of the wild oxen you have rescued me.
22 I will tell of your name to my brothers and sisters;
      in the midst of the congregation I will praise you:
23 You who fear the Lord, praise him! . . .
24 For he did not despise or abhor
      the affliction of the afflicted;
  he did not hide his face from me,
      but heard when I cried to him. . . .
27 All the ends of the earth shall remember
      and turn to the Lord; . . .
28 For dominion belongs to the Lord,
      and he rules over the nations.
29 To him, indeed, shall all who sleep in the earth
          bow down;
    before him shall bow all who go down to the dust,
    and I shall live for him.
30 Posterity will serve him;
      future generations will be told about the Lord,
31 and proclaim his deliverance to a people yet unborn,
    saying that he has done it.

10 minutes
Choose questions according to your interest and time.

1 What do the onlookers think is the purpose of Jesus' words in Mark 15:34?

2 What does the psalmist mean in verse 1 when he or she speaks of God abandoning him? (There is no simple answer to this question!)

3 Examine the sudden change from the first to the second half of Psalm 22:21. Compare this to the change in Psalm 69 from verse 29 to verse 30. What is the similarity between these two sudden transitions?

4 In Psalm 22:27–31, why will so many people besides the psalmist praise God?

5 What do this Gospel reading and this psalm tell us about the kind of person God is?

A Guide to the Reading

If participants have not read this section already, read it aloud. Otherwise go on to "Questions for Application."

In the Gospels, Jesus often quotes the psalms, but only as he dies do we hear him using the psalms as his prayers. In Luke's Gospel, with his last breath Jesus utters words from Psalm 31. In Matthew and Mark, he begins to pray Psalm 22. Jesus drew on the psalms in his suffering, just as many of us today turn to the psalms when we need prayers that help us express our pain and grief.

"My God, why have you forsaken me?" Jesus' cry from the cross sounds like an agonized discovery that God has in fact abandoned him, a shriek of despair aimed at a silent sky. These words have sometimes been interpreted as an indication that in his final moments Jesus realized that he had misunderstood God's will and that God had now abandoned him to his fate. Can this interpretation be correct?

One source of an answer is Psalm 22. Gasping for breath (crucifixion slowly asphyxiates the victim), Jesus was probably incapable of reciting the entire psalm. But he may well have had the whole psalm in his mind as he prayed its opening words.

Psalm 22. It must be obvious to any reader how appropriate a prayer Psalm 22 was for Jesus on the cross. These are the words of someone in extreme suffering. The psalmist is "groaning" (22:1)—the Hebrew word means roaring, bawling. Death is near—so near that the psalmist is already treated as dead: his clothing is being divided up (22:18). His suffering is not only physical but social: he is subjected to such gross humiliation that he seems no longer human. He is cast out of society, reduced to social nothingness (22:6).

Nevertheless, Psalm 22 is not a groan of despair. The psalmist does not describe his plight to express hopelessness but to move God to act on his behalf. Implicitly the psalmist is saying to God: "You are so compassionate! Surely you will help me if you see how greatly I am suffering." This logic leads the psalmist to remind God of his past kindness—how God formed him before birth, then acted as midwife, entrusting the newborn to the mother's breasts (22:9). Now that the psalmist is in agony, this kindly God should recognize his parental responsibilities! Similarly, the psalmist's recalling of God's past blessings to Israel is a reproach for God's present failure to save. "You aided Israel in days gone by. How, then, can you abandon me to my enemies?" (22:3–5). From verse 1 through verse 21 the psalmist makes a single-minded attempt to secure God's help.

In this context, the anguished question—"Why have you forsaken me?"—is not an expression of despair but the opening volley of the psalmist's pathetic, reproachful assault on God. The psalmist's intention is to stir God to act. The psalmist thinks of God as having gone far away and needing to be exhorted to notice the psalmist's sufferings so that he will come and save (22:11). The question of verse 1 reminds God of the central reason why he should help: "Because you are *my God*!" Hovering at the edge of despair, Psalm 22 is nevertheless a remarkable expression of trust in God. *Even at the point of death* the psalmist continues vigorously to persuade God to save!

And the psalmist is confident that God will hear him. In the depths of suffering, he already envisions the thanks he will offer when God saves him (22:21–31). The psalmist looks forward to the moment when he will declare that God, who initially ignored his groaning (22:1), finally heard (22:24); that God, who did not answer (22:2), finally answered (22:21 says literally, "From the horns of the wild oxen you have answered me"). The psalmist is certain that those who mock him and proclaim him abandoned by God (22:6–8) will be shown to be mistaken (22:24). Indeed, the psalmist expects that God will intervene on his behalf so dramatically that it will draw forth praise in Israel and in other nations, in the present and the future, among both the living and the dead (22:27–31)! Coming from one in agony, this confidence that God will act for him—and through him for the world—is truly astounding.

Psalm 22 illustrates the paradox that bitter suffering does not necessarily destroy hope. It illustrates too the other side of the paradox—that trust in God does not preserve us from the experience of divine abandonment. Health and well-being are God's gifts, expressions of his love, tokens of his presence. When sickness and loss deprive us of these blessings, like the psalmist we too cry out to God, "Where have you gone? Why have you left us in misery?"

Mark 15:24–37. Jesus' prayer on the cross shows us that he experienced both sides of the paradox. He felt the dreadful condition of abandonment by God. Yet, despite being stripped of any sign of God's care, he continued to hope in God. The one who cried out, "Why have you forsaken me?" felt that God had abandoned him. Yet he did not abandon God. In the agony of death, Jesus continued to address God as "my God." Taken from a psalm that pleads for God's help, Jesus' words expressed not despair but conviction that God would save him.

The bystanders at the cross correctly perceived that Jesus was crying out for help, although they misunderstood to whom he was calling. Mark reports that they interpreted Jesus' quotation of the first verse of Psalm 22 as a plea to Elijah (Mark 15:34–35; the Aramaic words for "my God" and "Elijah" are similar in sound). "Let us see whether Elijah will come to take him down," they said (Mark 15:36).

At some time in life, most of us undergo deep sorrow or pain. It might be comforting to think that if only our faith is great enough, we will be able to traverse these dark stretches of our earthly journey with a sustaining sense of God's presence. But Jesus' final prayer suggests that the experience of abandonment by God may also befall his followers. "My God, my God, why have you forsaken me?" is not the prayer of a sufferer who is wrapped in spiritual consolation but of someone from whom pain and grief have ripped away any sense of God's presence.

Yet if Jesus' experience demonstrates that perfect trust in God cannot shield us from the experience of desolation in our suffering, it also shows us that suffering by itself cannot extinguish that trust. On the cross, Jesus was deprived of any visible basis for hope. As he looked out from the cross, what results of his ministry could he see but rejection by his enemies and incomprehension by his friends? Yet as he died, he continued to pray. His quotation of Psalm 22 reveals an indestructible confidence that God would save him—and, through him, the rest of the human race. On the cross, Jesus experienced the torment of God's silence. By doing so, he showed us that the absence of God may be the most direct path into his presence, that God's failure to help may be the most effective means by which his purposes can be fulfilled.

Psalm 22 as our prayer. In Israel in the period before Jesus, when a person in need would come to the temple seeking God's help, a priest might suggest a fitting psalm to pray. If the afflicted one was in extreme sorrow or pain, the priest might recommend Psalm 22. For centuries, a long line of people had prayed this anguished prayer. In becoming human, God took his place in this line of sufferers. At Golgotha, he came to the front of the line; it was his turn to pray Psalm 22. By praying the psalm from the cross, Jesus identified himself with all those who suffer deeply. He joined those who are in the abyss of pain.

Jesus prayed Psalm 22 in his own agony; he is ready to pray this psalm with us in our time of Godforsakenness. As we pray Psalm 22, he puts his finger under the words that express trust in God. Jesus, the great pray-er of Psalm 22, shares with us his own confidence that God will answer our prayers of hope—if not in this present earthly life, then in his eternal kingdom.

If we think of the dying Jesus praying the first part of the psalm on the cross as a cry for deliverance (22:1–21), we may likewise picture him, risen, praying the second part of the psalm in heaven as a declaration of God's faithfulness (22:21–31). God answered Jesus' appeal from the cross not by rescuing him from death but by raising him up into everlasting life. As we pray Psalm 22:21–31, we may listen to these words as containing Jesus' encouragement to us: "See, God has answered my prayer for deliverance! You call on God now, trusting that he will answer your cries also!"

Questions for Application

40 minutes
Choose questions according to your interest and time.

1 How is Psalm 22 like or unlike your prayers in times of distress? What might you learn from this psalm about how to pray?

2 When has a time of suffering tested your faith in God? What was the outcome of this experience?

3 What helps a person grow in hope and trust in God?

4 When has someone accompanied you through a time of difficulty or suffering? How might this give you an insight into Jesus' relationship with you in times of distress? How might you become more aware of the support Jesus wants to give you?

5 The Israelite community prayed Psalm 22 with those who were in extreme suffering. How does your local community of faith help its suffering members turn to God? How does your community help sufferers experience Jesus' presence with them in their pain? How could your local community— and you yourself—grow in being present with those who are in sorrow or pain?

6 What lesson have you learned about being helpful to someone who is going through a period of pain or loss?

7 For personal reflection: What meaning does Jesus' suffering have for you? What is your response to his suffering for you?

It is important to listen always anew to the biblical message, in a way that is quite personal, as words directly addressed to me, as words that do not belong to the past but speak to me today.

Cardinal Joseph Ratzinger

Approach to Prayer

15 minutes
Use this approach—or create your own!

◆ Set up a crucifix. Let individual participants take turns reading the verses of Psalm 22. Allow a time for participants to express short, informal prayers of any sort. Close with a prayer of thanks.

A Living Tradition

Finding Jesus in Psalm 22

This section is a supplement for individual reading.

Psalm 22 has often been read as a detailed before-the-fact account of Jesus' crucifixion. St. Augustine, for example, writes: "Christ's passion is set forth as clearly here as in the Gospel." Augustine asks, "To what end did Jesus exclaim, 'My God, my God, why hast thou forsaken me?' except to draw our attention and tell us, 'This psalm is written about me'?"

Augustine read the entire psalm as the words of Christ on the cross. From verses 6 through 18, it seemed to Augustine that Christ was speaking directly of his torments. But at other points, Augustine had to explain how Christ could say things that do not seem to represent his condition. For example, thinking it impossible that Jesus would have experienced separation from God, Augustine interprets 22:1–5 as spoken by Jesus on behalf of sinful human beings: "He uttered a great cry, thus signifying the old self whose mortality he had assumed. . . . 'Thou art far from coming to my aid,' since salvation is far from sinners. . . . He who thus prays nailed to the cross is indeed our old self who does not even know why God has forsaken him. . . . He was speaking of me, of you, of the other person, for he was bearing with him his body, the church."

In the psalmist's declaration "you do not answer" (22:2), Augustine found a teaching purpose: "Many cry out in trouble and are not heard, but this is for their well-being and not to show their folly. Paul cried out to be rid of the sting of the flesh, yet he was not set free from it by way of reply; rather he was told: 'My grace is sufficient for thee.' . . . So Paul went unheard not to manifest his folly but to increase his wisdom, that man may understand that God is a physician, and trouble a saving remedy." Augustine did not think that Christ needed to learn this lesson. Rather, Augustine believed, he spoke these words for our sake so that we might learn that it is salutary for us that our prayers sometimes go unanswered.

Beginning with 22:22, Augustine heard Jesus speaking of the reason for his sufferings. He suffered so that "the furthest dwellers of earth will come back to the Lord."

Jesus' Favorite Psalms

Did Jesus have favorite psalms? Among the 150 psalms in the psalter, were there any that held a special attraction for him? And if so, did he teach his disciples the meaning that these psalms had for him?

The Gospels do not contain accounts of Jesus giving his followers instruction in the psalms, or even of him identifying particular psalms as having special importance for him. But the authors of the Gospels did not attempt to present everything that Jesus said and did (John 21:25). So the absence of Gospel episodes in which Jesus teaches his disciples about the psalms is not evidence against the possibility.

The Gospels do contain suggestions that Jesus gave his disciples instruction in how the psalms referred to him. Luke, for example, reports that after Jesus' resurrection he "opened their minds" to grasp how the biblical writings—"the law of Moses, the prophets, and the psalms"—spoke about his death and resurrection (Luke 24:44–46). It seems likely that Jesus would also have given this kind of instruction to his followers before his death.

A positive piece of evidence that Jesus gave such instruction during his ministry lies in the fact that a relative handful of psalms keep popping up in the Gospels and in other New Testament writings.

Take Psalm 2, for example. God's words to Jesus at his baptism allude to verse 7 ("You are my son"— Mark 1:11; Luke 3:22; compare Matthew 3:17). An allusion to this same verse appears when God speaks at Jesus' transfiguration (Matthew 17:5; Mark 9:7; Luke 9:35). The reminiscence of the transfiguration in 2 Peter likewise recalls this allusion to Psalm 2:7 (2 Peter 1:17). Paul explicitly cites the same psalm verse in his preaching about Jesus in the Acts of the Apostles (Acts 13:33). Finally, the letter to the Hebrews twice connects this psalm verse with Jesus (Hebrews 1:5; 5:5).

In addition, the New Testament contains quotations from or allusions to other verses of Psalm 2 (verse 1 in Revelation 11:18; verse 2 in Revelation 19:19; verses 1–2 in Acts 4:25–26; verse 8 in Hebrews 1:2; verse 9 in Revelation 12:5 and 19:15;

verses 8–9 in Revelation 2:26–27; and verse 11 in Philippians 2:12).

A similar pattern of widespread New Testament use occurs with Psalm 110 and, to a lesser degree, with the other psalms that we have read in this guide (Psalms 8, 22, 69, 118).

What is significant about these repeated New Testament references to certain psalms is that they are found in the writings of authors who wrote at different times and in different places and who probably did not have the opportunity to read one another's writings. The reliance of different authors on the same handful of psalms suggests that they drew on a common tradition that these psalms were especially important for understanding Jesus. It seems likely that this tradition arose at an early stage in the growth of the Church, before the Christian movement began to spread outward into different places. Quite possibly the tradition of connecting these particular psalms with Jesus developed before the gospel spread beyond Palestine.

Who developed this tradition of connecting these particular psalms with Jesus? The simplest explanation is that Jesus himself initiated this tradition. The reason that references to these psalms continued to echo throughout the writings of the early Church is that Jesus had already pointed his original followers to these psalms as especially important for understanding who he was and how he had come to accomplish his mission.

It requires only one further step of inference to reach the conclusion that Jesus focused on these psalms in his teaching because he himself had already focused on them in his own meditation and prayer.

This conclusion leads us to another question. Did these psalms guide Jesus toward an understanding of himself and his mission?

The idea of Jesus' learning is not ruled out by his divinity. The eternal Word of God knows all that God knows: all! Yet as the Word-made-flesh—as God become a human being—Jesus "increased in wisdom" in the natural process of growing up (Luke 2:52). As a human being, Jesus progressed from knowing God as a two year old to knowing him as a twelve year old, and then as a man of thirty. It is reasonable to suppose that Jesus' comprehension of himself and of his role in God's plans for the human race deepened as he matured. The psalms may well have played a part in his growth.

This is not to say that Jesus learned of his identity from the psalms. Consider, for example, God's statement in Psalm 2:7— "You are my son." This psalm could not *inform* Jesus that he was God's Son. He would have needed something outside the psalm (his divine self-knowledge) in order to know that the statement referred especially to him.

Likewise, Jesus could not have learned about his mission simply from the psalms, for the psalms do not provide a straight-forward, ready-made description of his mission. Various psalms, for example, indicate that God was going to designate a military-style king to restore his people by crushing their enemies on the battlefield and giving them an earthly kingdom. In Psalm 2, God commissions a king to "break" his enemies "with a rod of iron" (2:9). Yet Jesus never showed any doubt that he was to end his life by mounting a cross, not a throne. He could not have found this message in the psalms unless in some way he knew it already.

Jesus, then, did not passively absorb the message at the surface of the psalms. Rather, he penetrated to their deeper meaning on the basis of his profound insight into God and God's activity in the world. From his knowledge of God's mercy and love, Jesus realized that the psalms' references to military victory and political rule were not to be interpreted as literal descriptions of the coming of God's kingdom. Jesus took the psalms' references to kingship and conquest as images for the advance of God's saving presence in the world. He read the psalms' statements about shattering enemies as metaphors for the powerful manner in which God would save men and women from the grip of sin.

Jesus also brought to the psalms a knowledge that enabled him to recognize that certain psalms had a messianic significance that other Jews had not discovered. Jesus' fellow Jews did not regard psalms of innocent sufferers, such as Psalm 69, as having any particular significance with regard to God's saving plans. But Jesus' quotation of these psalms in the Gospels shows that he saw them as pointers to the path of suffering by which he would enter his kingdom. In these psalms Jesus saw the pattern of his own mission. He would suffer an unjustified execution, calling on God to save him. Then he would rise from the dead, and his resurrection, the supreme act of divine power, would overflow to the benefit of men and women everywhere.

It seems, then, that Jesus learned from the psalms through a process of creative interaction. Guided by his divine knowledge, he discerned in these ancient prayers of Israel the divine master plan to which they give shadowy testimony (see Luke 24:44; compare Hebrews 1:1–2).

We cannot follow Jesus through the steps by which he came to grasp the shape and difficulty of his mission, but we may suppose that it was not a comfortable process. Every foreshadowing of suffering that he found in the psalms would have confronted him anew with the challenge of whether he was willing to embrace his Father's plan. Jesus did always embrace his Father's will, but sometimes only through great inner struggle. At the beginning of his ministry, we see Jesus struggling with the temptation to use his extraordinary power to gain political ascendancy (see Matthew 4:1–11). Near the end of his life, we see him pleading with his Father to provide a detour around the cross (see Matthew 26:36–44). It is reasonable to think that this struggle to embrace his Father's will began earlier, during his years in Nazareth. Psalm 22 and Psalm 69 may have been a kind of Gethsemane before Gethsemane, where Jesus struggled to abandon himself to his Father's will.

If the psalms confronted Jesus with a message about the suffering that lay ahead of him, they also provided him with ways of expressing his acceptance of his part in God's plan of salvation despite the suffering it would entail. In the psalms, Jesus found words that expressed confidence in God's power, trust that his Father would not allow death to have the last word, hope that through him his Father would bring life to the human race. These are the meanings that we too may express to God as we pray these psalms as his disciples.

75

Suggestions for Bible Discussion Groups

Like a camping trip, a Bible discussion group works best if you agree on where you're going and how you intend to get there. Many groups use their first meeting to talk over such questions and reach a consensus. Here is a checklist of issues, with bits of advice from people who have experience in Bible discussions. (A planning discussion will go more smoothly if the leaders have thought through the following issues beforehand.)

Agree on your purpose. Are you getting together to gain wisdom and direction for your lives? to finally get acquainted with the Bible? to support one another in following Christ? to encourage those who are exploring—or reexploring—the Church? for other reasons?

Agree on attitudes. For example: "We're all beginners here." "We're here to help one another understand and respond to God's word." "We're not here to offer counseling or direction to one another." "We want to read Scripture prayerfully." What do *you* wish to emphasize? Make it explicit!

Agree on ground rules. Barbara J. Fleischer, in her useful book *Facilitating for Growth*, recommends that a group clearly state its approach to the following:

- *Preparation.* Do we agree to read the material and prepare answers to the questions before each meeting?
- *Attendance.* What kind of priority will we give to our meetings?
- *Self-revelation.* Are we willing to help the others in the group gradually get to know us—our weaknesses as well as our strengths, our needs as well as our gifts?
- *Listening.* Will we commit ourselves to listening to one another?
- *Confidentiality.* Will we keep everything that is shared *with* the group *in* the group?
- *Discretion.* Will we refrain from sharing about the faults and sins of people who are not in the group?
- *Encouragement and support.* Will we give as well as receive?
- *Participation.* Will we give each person the time and opportunity to make a contribution?

You could probably take a pen and draw a circle around *listening* and *confidentiality.* Those two points are especially important.

The following items could be added to Fleischer's list:

◆ *Relationship with parish.* Is our group part of the adult faith-formation program? independent but operating with the express approval of the pastor? not a parish-based group?

◆ *New members.* Will we let new members join us once we have begun the six weeks of discussions?

Agree on housekeeping.

◆ *When will we meet?*

◆ *How often will we meet?* Meeting weekly or every other week is best if you can manage it. William Riley remarks, "Meetings once a month are too distant from each other for the threads of the last session not to be lost" *(The Bible Study Group: An Owner's Manual).*

◆ *How long will meetings run?*

◆ *Where will we meet?*

◆ *Is any setup needed?* Christine Dodd writes that "the problem with meeting in a place like a church hall is that it can be very soul-destroying," given the cold, impersonal feel of many church facilities. If you have to meet in a church facility, Dodd recommends doing something to make the area homey *(Making Scripture Work).*

◆ *Who will host the meetings?* Leaders and hosts are not necessarily the same people.

◆ *Will we have refreshments?* Who will provide them? Don Cousins and Judson Poling make this recommendation: "Serve refreshments if you like, but save snacks and other foods for the end of the meeting to minimize distractions" *(Leader's Guide 1).*

◆ *What about child care?* Most experienced leaders of Bible discussion groups discourage bringing infants or other children to adult Bible discussions.

Agree on leadership. You need someone to facilitate— to keep the discussion on track, to see that everyone has a chance to speak, to help the group stay on schedule. Rena Duff, editor of the newsletter *Sharing God's Word Today,* recommends having two or three people take turns leading the discussions.

It's okay if the leader is not an expert on the Bible. You have this booklet, and if questions come up that no one can answer, you can delegate a participant to do a little research between meetings. It's important for the leader to set an example of listening, to draw out the quieter members (and occasionally restrain the more vocal ones), to move the group on when it gets stuck, to remind the members of their agreements, and to summarize what the group is accomplishing.

Bible discussion is an opportunity to experience the fulfillment of Jesus' promise "Where two or three are gathered in my name, I am there among them" (Matthew 18:20). Put your discussion group in Jesus' hands. Pray for the guidance of the Spirit. And have a great time exploring God's word together!

Y ou can use this booklet just as well for individual study as for group discussion. While discussing the Bible with other people can be a rich experience, there are advantages to reading on your own. For example:

◆ You can focus on the points that interest you most.

◆ You can go at your own pace.

◆ You can be completely relaxed and unashamedly honest in your answers to all the questions, since you don't have to share them with anyone!

My suggestions for using this booklet on your own are these:

◆ Don't skip the Questions to Begin. The questions can help you as an individual reader warm up to the topic of the reading.

◆ Take your time on the Questions for Careful Reading and Questions for Application. While a group will probably not have enough time to work on all the questions, you can allow yourself the time to consider all of them if you are using the booklet by yourself.

◆ After reading the Guide to the Reading, go back and reread the Scripture text before answering the Questions for Application.

◆ Take the time to look up all the parenthetical Scripture references.

◆ Since you control the pace, give yourself plenty of opportunities to reflect on the meaning of the psalms and Gospel passages for you. Let your reading be an opportunity for these words to become God's words to you.

Resources

Bibles

The following editions of the Bible contain the full set of biblical books recognized by the Catholic Church, along with a great deal of useful explanatory material:

- The Catholic Study Bible (Oxford University Press), which uses the text of the New American Bible
- The Catholic Bible: Personal Study Edition (Oxford University Press), which also uses the text of the New American Bible
- The New Jerusalem Bible, the regular or standard (not the reader's) edition (Doubleday)

Books

- Roland E. Murphy, *The Psalms Are Yours* (New York: Paulist Press, 1993).
- Irene Nowell, *Sing a New Song: The Psalms in the Sunday Lectionary* (Collegeville, Minn.: Liturgical Press, 1993).
- Thomas Merton, *Bread in the Wilderness* (Collegeville, Minn.: Liturgical Press, 1986).

How has Scripture had an impact on your life? Was this booklet helpful to you in your study of the Bible? Please send comments, suggestions, and personal experiences to Kevin Perrotta, General Editor, Trade Editorial Department, Loyola Press, 3441 N. Ashland Ave., Chicago, IL 60657.